The Apostles' Creed

Adult Coloring Book

The Complete Text of the Apostles' Creed in Large, Simple Coloring Font with 20 Cross Coloring Pages

ESTHER PINCINI

The Apostles' Creed Adult Coloring Book
The Complete Text of the Apostles' Creed in Large, Simple Coloring Font
with 20 Cross Coloring Pages

by Esther Pincini

ISBN 978-1-77335-096-7

Magdalene Press, 2016

1.

I believe in God the Father,

Almighty, Maker of heaven and earth:

2.

And in Jesus Christ, his only

begotten Son, our Lord:

3.

Who was conceived by the Holy

Ghost, born of the Virgin Mary:

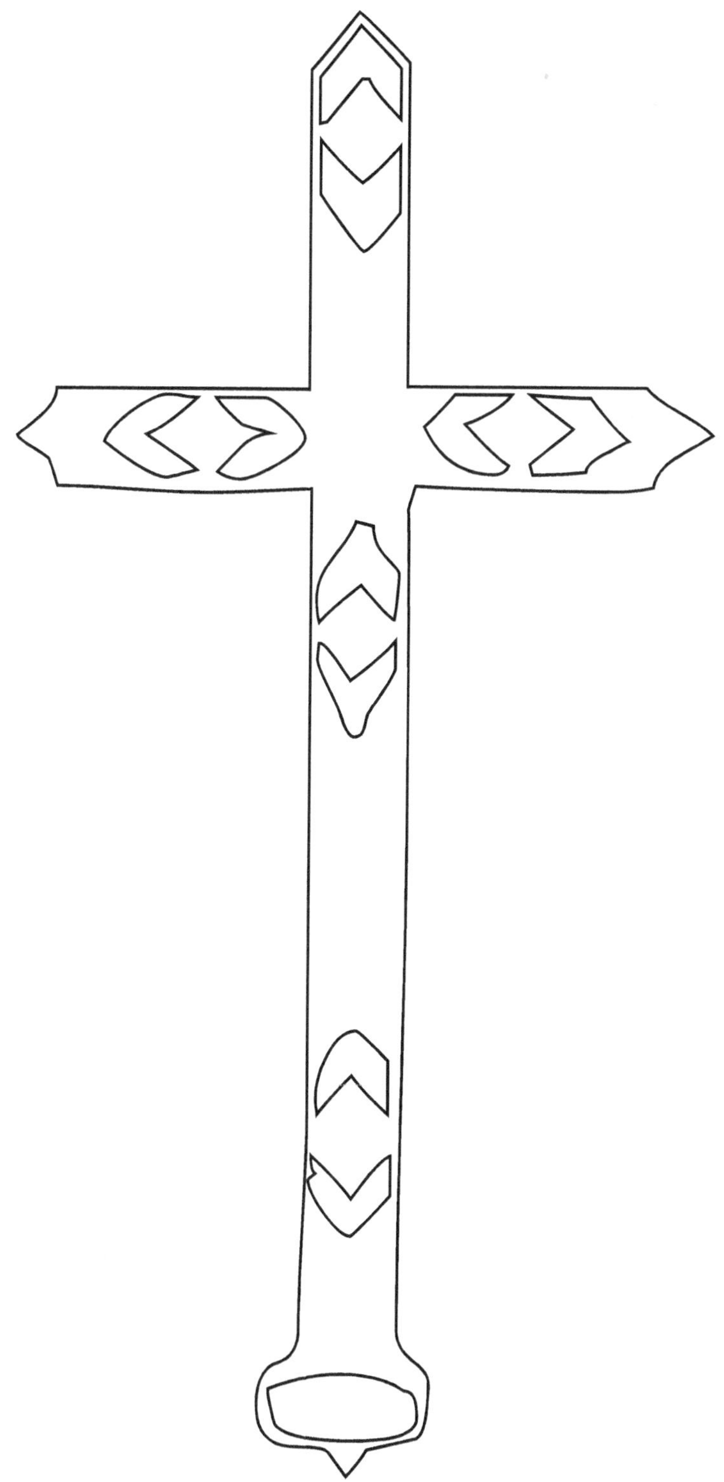

4.

Suffered under Pontius Pilate; was

crucified,
dead and
buried: He
descended
into hell:

5.

The third day he rose again from the dead:

6.

He ascended into heaven, and sits at

the right hand of God the Father Almighty:

7.

From thence he shall come

to judge
the quick
and the
dead:

8.

I believe in the Holy Ghost:

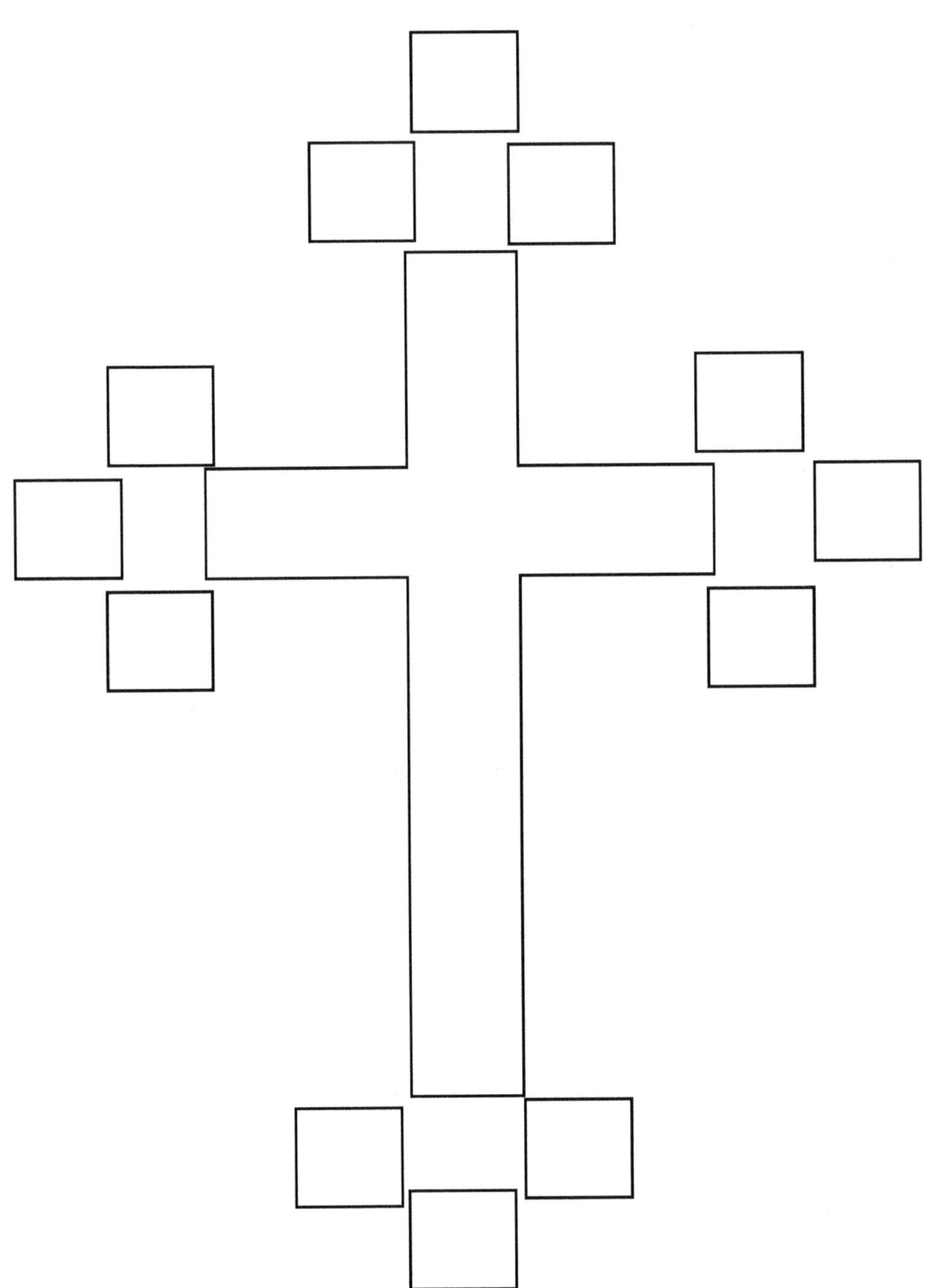

9.

I believe in the holy catholic

church: the communion of saints:

10.

The forgiveness of sins:

11.

The resurrection of the body:

12.

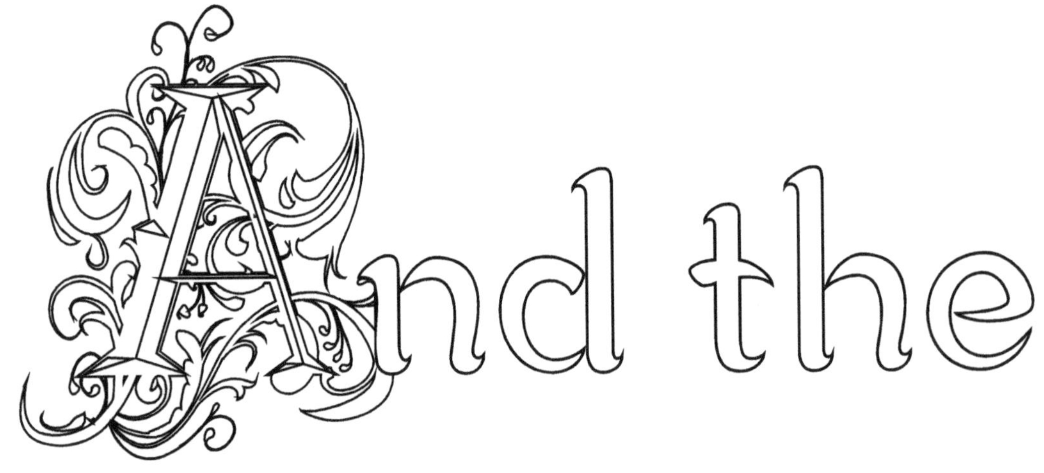

And the life everlasting.

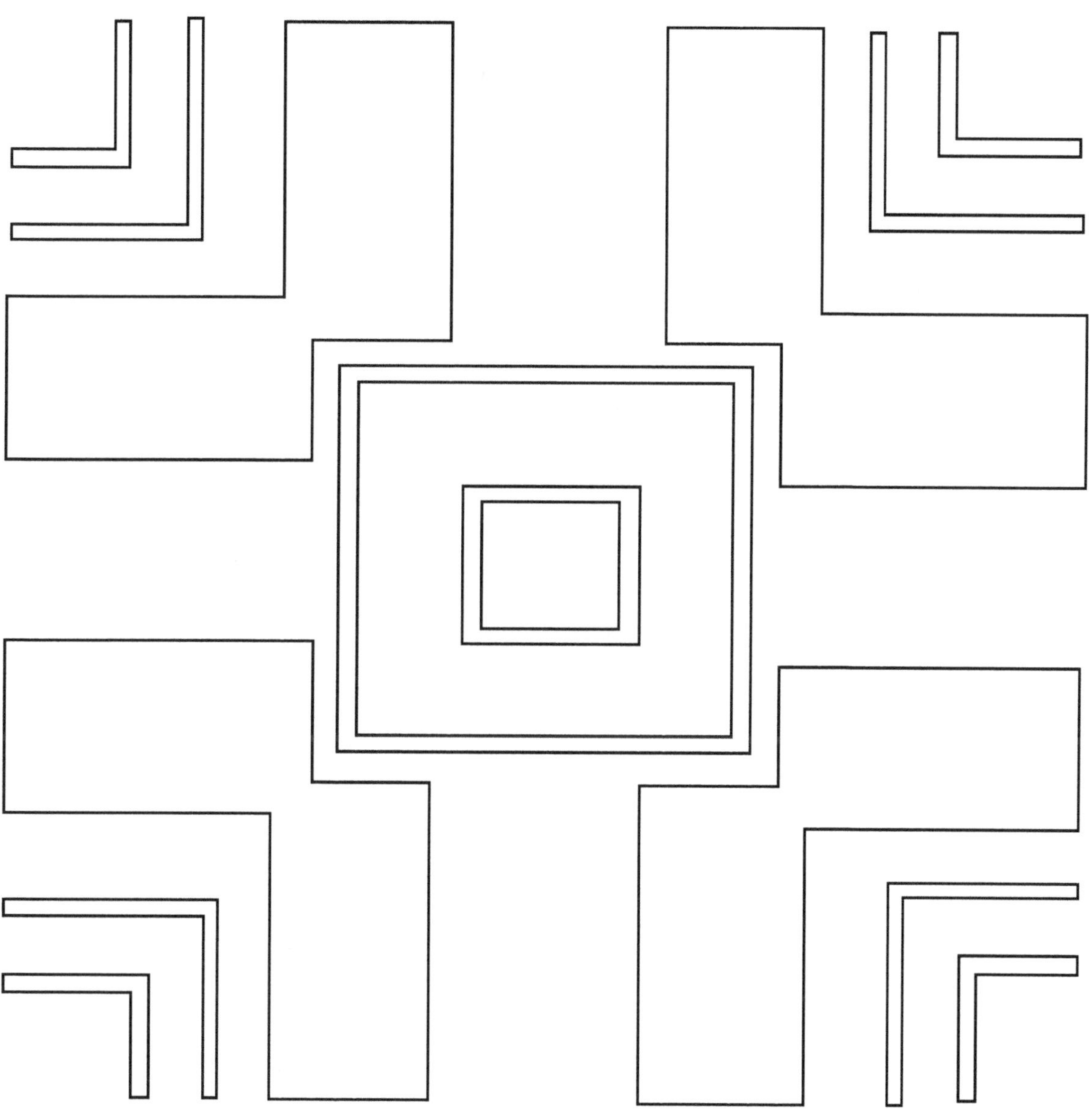

Amen.

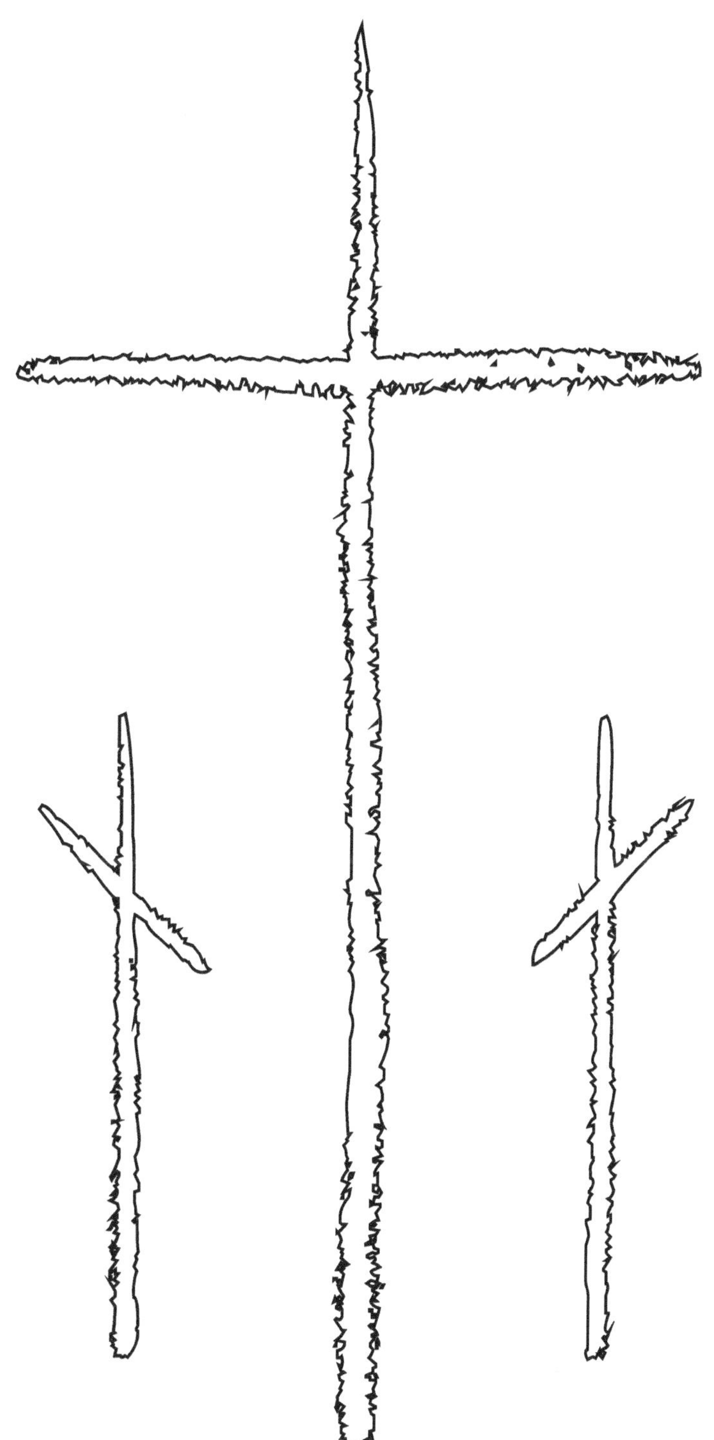

www.ingramcontent.com/pod-product-compliance
Lightning Source LLC
Chambersburg PA
CBHW081228040426
42445CB00016B/1917

* 9 7 8 1 7 7 3 3 5 0 9 6 7 *